CW01082685

Original title:

Way to Yourself

Editor: Jessica Elisabeth Luik

Author: Kene Elistrand

ISBN HARDBACK: 978-9916-86-056-4

ISBN PAPERBACK: 978-9916-86-057-1

Journey into the Soul

With every step, the light does grow
Into the depths we dare to go
Within the heart, a secret space
Where shadows dance, and fears embrace

A mirror clear, with truth untold
Reflections brave, both young and old
We wander through the mist and rain
To find the joy amidst the pain

A whisper calls from far within
A healing balm for all our sin
In silence deep, the answers lie
Beneath the earth, beyond the sky

Unfolding the Inner Map

Paths converge in twilight's grace
A map unfolds in quiet pace
The silent stars, they guide the way
Through night's embrace and break of day

Each journey starts from the unseen
The mind's expanse so vast and keen
To navigate the heart's terrain
Weize each loss and cherish gain

Signs etched in dreams, by night's soft gleam
In stillness find the hidden seam
A compass spun by hands so wise
Leads straight through storms, beneath the skies

Whispers of True Being

Voices soft in twilight's fold
Secrets gently shared, retold
In sacred space, where spirits blend
A tender guide, the soul's true friend

Unmask the self, unveil the mind
In truth, we seek, in heart we find
Through quiet woods and bending streams
We chase the echoes of our dreams

Listen deep to nature's call
In whispered breaths, we hear it all
A song that's sung beyond the veil
In true being, we shall prevail

Steps towards Awakening

With each new dawn, a chance to rise
To see the world with clearer eyes
Awaking from the night's embrace
To feel the sun upon our face

Steps taken slow, with mindful care
A path of grace that leads us there
Through valleys dark and mountains high
We find the truth that's nestled nigh

The heart's own drum, it beats in time
With rhythms pure, and songs sublime
In waking state, our souls expand
To grasp the light with open hand

My Own Horizon

Beneath the vast expanse, I stand alone,
Dreams weave the sky in colors unknown,
Stars whisper secrets, fragile and bright,
Guiding my heart through the silent night.

The ocean's embrace, a symphony of waves,
Charting my course to uncharted caves,
Each crest and trough, a tale to unfold,
In the depths of my soul, stories told.

Mountains rise tall, guardians of time,
Whispering winds, a melodious chime,
As I climb higher, through clouds I soar,
Finding myself at my own horizon's door.

Veins of Tranquility

In forests deep, where shadows lay,
Streams of serenity guide the way,
Through veins of crystal, life's essence flows,
Nourishing dreams where tranquility grows.

Leaves rustle softly, secrets they keep,
Of mornings kissed by sunlight's sweep,
In this refuge, where spirits unite,
Harmony dances with pure delight.

Birdsong weaves melodies fine,
Threads of peace in each line,
Binding hearts with nature's art,
In tranquil veins, we find our part.

Canyon of Contemplation

Carved by the ages, silent and grand,
A canyon whispers across the land,
Echoes of thoughts in shadows gleam,
A timeless realm where minds can dream.

The river winds with questions bold,
In ancient grooves, true stories told,
Among the cliffs, answers reside,
Within the silence, where doubts abide.

Under the sky, open and wide,
I walk the path where secrets hide,
In this canyon of contemplation,
I find reflection, and revelation.

The Quiet Rift

Between the world and dreams of mind,
A quiet rift, serene and kind,
Whispers of thoughts in twilight's grace,
Where shadows dance and stars embrace.

Softly the night folds wings of peace,
In that rift, all struggles cease,
Harmony drapes with gentle hands,
Guiding hearts to calmer lands.

In this place, where stillness reigns,
Wisdom flows through silent plains,
A realm where souls can drift,
Within the calm of the quiet rift.

Veil of My Essence

Through wisps of time, my soul does wade
In dreams where hopes and fears parade
A whisper lost in subtle shade
A silhouette, a masquerade

Beneath the night, my thoughts take flight
A glimmered dance in pale moonlight
What shadows hide, what truths ignite
In silent realms, a heart's delight

A tapestry of breath and sighs
Woven threads of low and highs
In quiet beats my spirit lies
A mirror where my essence cries

Underneath the Silence.

In hush of dawn, the world holds still
A heart awaits its silent thrill
The morning mist, a tender chill
Whispers secrets, soft and nil

Below the surface, currents move
A symphony that needs no proof
The quiet hum, a hidden groove
A time for souls to find their truth

In silence deep, we come undone
A journey bound but just begun
The quiet sky, the setting sun
Embrace the calm where minds can run

Path of Inner Light

A lantern bright within the soul
Illuminates the unseen goal
Where shadows dwell and echoes toll
A light that makes the spirit whole

Through winding roads of night's embrace
A glow that guides with gentle grace
An inner spark, a sacred place
Where dreams align and fears efface

A beacon in the darkest hour
A blossom bright, a hidden flower
In quiet strength, we feel the power
A light within that cannot cower

Echoes of Self-Discovery

In chambers vast within the mind
A map of stars that intertwine
Each echo is a path defined
A journey carved through space and time

A whisper from the depths within
Reveals the place where dreams begin
In silence breaks the softest din
Where true reflection does not thin

A path revealed, a self regained
Through echoed steps, through tears and rain
In mirrors clear, no loss, no gain
But wholeness found through tender pain

Odyssey of the Mind

In realms where thoughts do freely roam,
Imagination finds its home.
Through corridors of dreams we wind,
An endless odyssey of mind.

Uncharted maps on mental seas,
Where concepts float like autumn leaves.
In shadows deep and dreams confined,
An endless odyssey of mind.

Each idea births a vivid hue,
A sunset's glow, a morning dew.
In endless loops of space and time,
An endless odyssey of mind.

Nurturing the Inner Flame

Within the heart a spark resides,
A flame that through the darkness guides.
With tender care and gentle aim,
We nurture well our inner flame.

Through trials harsh and storms so wild,
This light remains both fierce and mild.
In quiet strength without a name,
We nurture well our inner flame.

In every breath that we intake,
This fire we keep, this fire we make.
Though life itself may be a game,
We nurture well our inner flame.

Silhouettes of Self

Reflections cast, the twilight calls,
In shadows on the dusky walls.
A tumult of the heart and health,
We trace the silhouettes of self.

In mirrored pools where fears reside,
And virtues in the silence hide.
With every joy and sorrow felt,
We trace the silhouettes of self.

Through nights of dreams and dawns of truth,
In age and in the bloom of youth.
In every loss, each timeless wealth,
We trace the silhouettes of self.

Resonance in Silence

In quiet moments deeply found,
When no one speaks, there is no sound.
An echo whispers, soft, profound,
The resonance in silence bound.

Through tranquil seas and calm we float,
On waves of thought in dreamlike boats.
A stillness in the soul's deep moat,
The resonance in silence wrote.

The breath of night, the hush of day,
In silent words we find our way.
An open space, a blank rich note,
The resonance in silence dotes.

Inner Mystical Quest

Through shadows deep, the spirit strives,
In realms where dreams and daylight blend.
A journey cloaked in silent sighs,
Where hearts and whispers comprehend.

In winding paths where secrets dwell,
With ancient trees that softly speak,
The soul unfurls, its tale to tell,
In moments lost, yet far from weak.

Beyond the veil, the future calls,
To seek the truths that lie within.
As night descends, as daylight falls,
The quest for light and life begins.

Echoes of the Inner Trail

In twilight's hush, the echoes rise,
A symphony of silent sound.
Through unseen glades, where truth abides,
The heart encased in glories found.

With every step in shadowed light,
The whispers of the past collide.
A dance of time, both dark and bright,
In echoes where our dreams reside.

Through winding trails of inner lore,
Where fears and hopes in tandem weave.
The heart becomes forevermore,
A song of faith we can't conceive.

Following the Soul's Guide

Deep within, a spark ignites,
Guiding the heart through unknown seas.
Past whispered winds and starry nights,
To realms where only courage sees.

The spirit moves in gentle grace,
Following paths where shadows play.
A silent dance, an endless chase,
Towards dawn's first light, where dreams array.

In every wind and whispered wave,
The soul discerns the ancient charts.
Through doubt's domain and hope's enclave,
A journey true that binds our hearts.

Inner Radiance Path

Beneath the stars, the spirit shines,
An inner light that leads the way.
Through night's embrace and cosmic signs,
We tread the dawn of a new day.

In realms where silence softly sings,
The heart's own radiance reveals.
A journey crowned by unseen wings,
Through timeless worlds our fate appeals.

Upon the path where shadows blend,
A luminance begins to rise.
With every step, the soul will mend,
By light within and endless skies.

Hidden Layers

Beneath the surface, shadows play,
Veils of secrets softly sway.
Moments lost, that time betrays,
In hidden layers, dreams do lay.

Whispers find their sacred sleep,
In the place where echoes weep.
Silent currents, running deep,
unlocking truths, histories keep.

Thoughts like rivers carve the stone,
In the quiet, seeds are sown.
Hidden layers, left unknown,
Where our souls, in twilight, roam.

Uncharted Depths

In the deep where darkness dwells,
Mysteries weave their silent spells.
Untold stories, secret wells,
Within uncharted depths, magic swells.

Lost in oceans of the mind,
Treasures rare and undefined.
Hidden gems for us to find,
Through the currents, fate aligned.

Midnight whispers guide the way,
Into night, the brave will stray.
In the depth's eternal stay,
Hidden worlds in shadows play.

Sanctuary of Thoughts

In the quiet, minds do grow,
Sanctuaries we still don't know.
Seeds of wisdom, hearts do sow,
Within realms where thoughts may flow.

In those corners, soft and warm,
Ideas gather, thoughts transform.
Safe from chaos, far from harm,
Sanctuary's sweet, calming charm.

Dreams take flight on gentle breeze,
In this tranquil mind's release.
Here we find our purest peace,
Where the whispering mind's disease.

The Inner Voyage

Set adrift on thoughts so wide,
Infinite seas where dreams reside.
Soulful tides we'll turn and tide,
On the inner voyage, side by side.

Charting stars unseen by night,
Guided by a quieter light.
Silent revelations tight,
In the journey's hush and sight.

To the heart's core we descend,
On this path where stories blend.
Inner voyage, without end,
Here, in solitude, we mend.

Vault of Resolve

In the depth of night's embrace,
We find our strength within,
A vault of quiet grace,
Where new resolve begins.

Through shadows deep and wide,
Hope flickers like a flame,
Guiding hearts that cannot hide,
From destiny's true name.

With courage as our guide,
We journey through the dark,
In every tear we've cried,
We forge a brighter spark.

For in the vault of soul,
Resilience does reside,
A whisper making us whole,
Eternal, undenied.

Resonating Silence

In the hush of morning light,
A symphony does play,
Silence resonates in might,
Inviting us to stay.

No words need to be spoken,
The stillness tells it all,
With bonds of peace unbroken,
We rise where shadows fall.

In moments pure and clear,
Our souls begin to speak,
The echoes we hold dear,
Are answers that we seek.

Listen to the silence,
It sings of love and peace,
A melody's reliance,
On quiet's sweet release.

The Essence Within

Beyond the mask of sorrow,
Lies beauty deep and true,
A promise of tomorrow,
In every heartfelt view.

Beneath the layers worn,
A spirit ever bright,
In hardship, dreams are born,
An unextinguished light.

Each heartbeat tells a tale,
Of love and loss and gain,
In trials, we prevail,
Resilient through the pain.

For essence dwells within,
Unseen by naked eyes,
A journey we begin,
Toward destiny's bright skies.

Reflections in the Stillness

In the stillness of the lake,
Reflections clear and bright,
A mirror for our sake,
To see with inner sight.

The world in quiet pause,
Reveals its hidden face,
No need for grand applause,
To know our rightful place.

With gentle heart, we find,
A peace that softly flows,
The solitude reminds,
Of truths that silence knows.

In every quiet mirror,
A deeper self is shown,
Reflections growing clearer,
When we are still alone.

Wellspring of My Being

Deep within, where shadows merge
A wellspring rises, pure and clear
Whispers of my spirit's urge
In silent moments, reappear

From caverns dark, the waters flow
Eternal tides of hope and grace
Life's essence, in gentle glow
Reflecting every somber face

In midnight's sweep, the calm persists
Beneath the turmoil, peace retains
A place where hidden joy exists
And love remains, despite the pains

As dawn unravels night's attire
This wellspring shines, a guiding light
Uplifting warmth, a soul on fire
Through endless days, and endless night

Wellspring of my being, rise
Gift me strength, and open skies

Embrace of the Inner Wind

Beneath the hush of twilight's grace
A whispering wind begins to play
Caressing thoughts in quiet space
And gently lifts the heart's dismay

The inner breeze, so soft and fair
Sweeps through the chambers of the soul
It dances light, it clears the air
And makes fragmented spirits whole

From deepest wells to open fields
This breath of life pursues the quest
And every healing touch it wields
Is cast upon the weary chest

In tender gusts, it finds its way
Through dreams, desires, sorrow's spin
It guides, it soothes, it will not stray
The sacred embrace of the wind

A dance unseen, yet deeply felt
Through trials, it bids the ice to melt

Labyrinth of Dreams

Lost within the midnight's maze
A dance of shadows, pale and soft
In dreams, the soul in silence lays
Where whispers echo clear, aloft

The labyrinth twists, in winding paths
Each corner hides a secret gleam
Revealing truths in sudden casts
Of moonlight's gentle, silver beam

Journey slow, through veils of time
Unraveling the woven thread
Of memories that pantomime
Life's woven tales, and hopes unfed

In every turn, a dream unfolds
A breath, a sigh, a fleeting glance
Through these halls, the spirit molds
The essence of the midnight dance

Labyrinth of dreams, you tease
With mysteries, that never cease

Silhouette of the Soul

In twilight's hue, a figure stands
A silhouette against the void
The soul, in gentle, graceful bands
Of light and shadow, unalloyed

Contours fade, yet essence shines
Through darkened night and dawning day
A presence felt in subtle signs
Unspoken words that find their way

The silhouette, a silent guide
Through realms unseen, it leads the way
In shadows deep, it does confide
The hidden truths of light's display

In whispers, soft, it calls my name
A beckoning from realms afar
A kindred light in shadow's frame
A soul's true self, a guiding star

Silhouette of soul, you stand
A beacon bright, in shadow land

Unveiling the Heart's Path

In shadows deep where secrets hide,
A lantern's glow, the heart's true guide,
Through twilight dreams and whispered sighs,
An inner world begins to rise.

Step softly now on paths unknown,
Where courage blooms and fears are sown,
The journey weaves through hopes and dreads,
A tapestry in golden threads.

With every beat, with every breath,
The spirit quests beyond mere death,
To find a realm where love remains,
Unchained by grief, unscarred by pains.

The Quest Within

Beneath the stars, in silent night,
A soul embarks on endless flight,
Through realms unseen and heights unfound,
In search of truths that world confound.

Echoes of past and dreams of new,
In labyrinths of thought pursue,
The glow of wisdom's gentle flame,
Guide steps unseen, unknown the name.

Each journey's end, a door ajar,
Reveals the self, both near and far,
The quest within, forevermore,
Unfolds its tale, a boundless lore.

In Search of Essence

Through veils of mist and time's embrace,
A soul seeks out its truest place,
Beyond the masks and silent fears,
Into the light where truth appears.

Each step unveils a hidden part,
Unfolding gently from the heart,
The essence pure, unchained by lies,
Reflects in each awoken eye.

In moments fraught with echoes deep,
The soul does rise from shadows' keep,
To touch the thread of life's intent,
In search of essence, heaven-sent.

Discovering Inner Horizons

Horizons vast, inside they lie,
Where dreams ascend and spirits fly,
Through valleys deep and mountains tall,
The heart's own journey, heed the call.

In twilight's hue and dawn's first light,
Begins the quest, dispels the night,
With every step, an inner sight,
Expands the view, ignites the fight.

Unveil the skies within the soul,
To find where life's true rivers roll,
Discovering horizons rare,
A boundless world, beyond compare.

Between Shadows and Light

In twilight's embrace, a dance we play,
Between shadows and light, we sway.
Fleeting whispers of dawn's first ray,
Night's curtain lifts, the dreams hold sway.

Darkness yields to morning's glow,
Secrets hidden, now they show.
In the balance of day and night,
We find our path, our guiding light.

Shadows fade as sun ascends,
Warding off the night's dark bends.
In this realm, where contrasts meet,
Every step feels bittersweet.

Light and dark, a timeless duet,
Every dawn, a new vignette.
In this realm of grey and bright,
We journey on, with hearts alight.

Lattice of Memory

Threads of gold and silver weave,
In the lattice, we believe.
Moments caught in time's own sieve,
Memories that we retrieve.

Echoes of a distant past,
In this web, our lives are cast.
Fragile whispers, shadows vast,
In this mesh, we're held steadfast.

Glimpses of a day gone by,
In this net, emotions lie.
Laughter, tears, a tender sigh,
Held within, we can't deny.

In this lattice, time stands still,
Every memory, a drill.
Woven tales our hearts fulfill,
Memory whispers, soft and shrill.

Introspection's Dance

In the silence of the mind,
Thoughts and dreams, they intertwine.
Paths we've taken, tales refined,
Seeking truths we hope to find.

Mirror's gaze, it meets our eyes,
Self-reflection, no disguise.
In this dance, the spirit flies,
Searching through life's tangled ties.

Questions linger in the dusk,
Mysteries we dare to unmask.
In the silence, voices husk,
Inward journeys, we will task.

Introspection's dance, so true,
Endless steps, a path to you.
In our hearts, the rhythm grew,
Guiding us to skies anew.

Luminous Shadows

Shadows dance in moonlit hall,
Luminous whispers, phantom call.
In the night, they softly fall,
Guided by the silver thrall.

Ephemeral lights, they gleam,
Casting shadows on a dream.
Floating through a midnight stream,
In their glow, we find a theme.

In the stillness, forms arise,
Shadows wane 'neath starry skies.
In their dance, the essence lies,
Secrets caught in night's demise.

Light and dark, a mystic blight,
Twisting forms in endless flight.
In their embrace, pure delight,
Luminous shadows, soft as night.

Inner Sanctum Chronicles

In whispers, twilight courts our soul,
A dance of shadows, faint and whole.
Silent echoes fill our mind,
Lost in secrets, hard to find.

Memories painted in hues of gold,
Stories ancient, yet untold.
Through realms unseen, we take our flight,
Guided by the inner light.

A sanctuary of thoughts profound,
In quiet space, where peace is found.
On wings of dreams, we glide, we soar,
To hidden temples, and so much more.

Emotions flow like rivers deep,
In the silence, we softly weep.
Each tear a verse in life's grand song,
In this sanctum, where we belong.

Contours of Identity

In the mirror, faces change,
A shifting canvas, vast and strange.
Echoes of a past we see,
Each one a piece of you and me.

Layers upon layers, we unfold,
Stories in our veins, so bold.
Ink of life, on skin it flows,
In patterns only we disclose.

Journeys taken, dreams once held,
In every scar, a tale expelled.
Together formed by time's caress,
Each contour shaped by tenderness.

In shadows cast by setting sun,
We find we're many, yet still one.
In every glance, we redefine,
The contours of a self divine.

Solitude's Serenade

Under moonlight's silver glow,
In quiet realms where spirits go.
Solitude sings a gentle song,
In those moments, we belong.

The night whispers in softest tones,
Amidst the stars, we are not alone.
In the silences so profound,
A deeper harmony is found.

Through winds that whisper tales unsaid,
And dreams that dance inside our head.
Solitude's serenade we hear,
In every note, we're drawn near.

Peace in shadows, calm in night,
A tranquil heart takes quiet flight.
In solitude, we find our grace,
A serenade, a safe embrace.

Mapping the Mind

Through labyrinths of thoughts we tread,
A map of dreams by courage led.
In corners dark, and spaces bright,
Mapping mind's intricate flight.

Stars of insight light our way,
Guiding through both night and day.
In constellations, stories weave,
Each thread a path we believe.

Fragments of a world unseen,
Places where we've never been.
Every twist and every turn,
A lesson learned, a wisdom earned.

In seas of thought, we chart our quest,
Through storms we face and trials we best.
Mapping the mind's vast expanse,
In every thought, a new chance.

Selfhood's Serene Walk

Beneath the sky so vast and blue,
I tread the path that's calm and true,
In the whispering leaves, I find my peace,
Nature's gentle touch, my soul's release.

With every step, my heart feels light,
In solitude, the world's just right,
No rush, no haste, just present grace,
A tranquil journey, a sacred space.

The breeze that guides, the sun that warms,
In quiet moments, my spirit forms,
A life unfurled in silent talk,
On selfhood's path, I softly walk.

Awakening the Inner Spirit

In dawn's first light, a whisper calls,
A gentle nudge beyond the walls,
The spirit stirs, it seeks the light,
Emerging from the heart's deep night.

With steady breath and calm embrace,
It finds the courage, seeks its place,
Awakening with bold intent,
A journey inward, soul's ascent.

Through silent prayers and quiet dreams,
The soul awakens, truth redeems,
In every beat, in every sigh,
The spirit soars, unbound, to fly.

Unwritten Inner Odyssey

A blank page, the start of dreams,
Where nothing's quite the way it seems,
A journey inward, penned by heart,
Each step a masterpiece of art.

In silent thoughts, the tale unfolds,
A quest for truths that time holds,
Through valleys deep and mountains high,
An odyssey where spirits fly.

No map, no guide to lead the way,
Just inner whispers, come what may,
An unwritten saga, vast and free,
The soul's own path, its destiny.

Silent Footsteps Within

In hollow echoes of the mind,
Silent footsteps, secrets find,
A quiet walk through thoughts unspoken,
Where silent dreams remain unbroken.

Each step, a memory, soft and near,
A journey brief, devoid of fear,
Within the shadows, truth does gleam,
In silent realms, where souls convene.

With gentle stride and calm repose,
A path unwinds, the spirit knows,
In silence deep, the heart's akin,
To peaceful walks, those steps within.

Unveiling the Inner Path

Upon the silent morning's breath,
In fields where shadows play,
I find the road concealed within,
And let it guide my way.

The whispering trees align my steps,
With secrets old and wise,
Through tangled woods and hidden bends,
The path before me lies.

Beneath the celestial lights' embrace,
In harmony I tread,
The journey of the heart unfolds,
By unseen hands I'm led.

Each footfall sings of worlds undone,
A tale both bright and vast,
With every turn, a story told,
Of futures and of past.

In stillness, the inner path reveals,
Its truths serene and near,
A conduit to the soul's desires,
Beyond the realm of fear.

Reflections in Quietude

In quietude, the night descends,
And wraps the world in peace,
The din of day, now softly fades,
Its clamor finds release.

The moonlight on the rippling pond,
A mirror to the sky,
Reflects the thoughts in silent minds,
That gently drift and lie.

Among the stars, the silence speaks,
In whispers soft and clear,
Of dreams and sighs and fervent hopes,
All held in tender care.

The leaves that fall in autumn's breath,
They pirouette and spin,
In stillness, they reveal their tale
Of journeys walked within.

Embracing quietude, we find,
A solace deep and true,
Reflections of our hearts entwined,
In moments pure and new.

Echoes of the Soul

In caverns deep within the heart,
Reside the echoes strong,
Of ancient tales and whispered dreams,
A soft, eternal song.

Each note resounds with memories,
Of laughter, tears, and days,
It paints the canvas of the soul,
In endless, vibrant ways.

Beneath the surface, ripples spread,
From joys and sorrows past,
Creating patterns, silent waves,
In echoes, they are cast.

Within the silent echoes' weave,
Lie truths that gently speak,
Of love and loss, of hope and faith,
In voices mild and meek.

The soul's deep echoes resonate,
Through time and space they roam,
A symphony of life's pure notes,
That always guide us home.

Whispers of My Heart

In tender whispers of my heart,
A language soft and true,
It speaks of love and dreams and fears,
In shades of every hue.

The murmurs of a twilight breeze,
They tell of days gone by,
Of moments stitched in memories,
Like stars in evening sky.

Each gentle beat, a story told,
Of passions held so dear,
The heart's own voice in quiet tones,
Sings melodies sincere.

Through whispers shared in silence deep,
Our souls are intertwined,
In rhythms pure and delicate,
Our hearts' sweet truths combined.

Within the whispers of my heart,
I hear your echoed song,
A symphony of love's embrace,
Where both our hearts belong.

Journey to the Core

Beneath the skies where dreams ascend,
Through paths unknown our spirits blend,
The stars like whispers murmur low,
Guiding hearts where rivers flow.

In shadows cast by moonlit air,
We seek the truths so pure, so rare,
A compass borne of ancient lore,
We journey to the mystic core.

Mountains high and valleys deep,
Secrets guard, in silence keep,
Each step a tale we write anew,
A voyage bound to what is true.

With every breath and every sigh,
We chart the stars within the sky,
In worlds unseen, our souls restore,
On this sacred journey to the core.

Inward Bound

Paths converge where heartstrings call,
Echoes dance along the hall,
In stillness, find the unknown sound,
A voyage casts - we're inward bound.

Mirrors face the soul within,
Reflecting light where dreams begin,
A labyrinth of hope unfound,
We venture forth, so inward bound.

Through the whispers of the mind,
Treasures lost, we hope to find,
In shadows deep, the spirits drown,
But strength renews, we're inward bound.

With patience, tread the silent night,
Till dawn reveals the hidden light,
The soul's true call will then resound,
And herald forth the inward bound.

Labyrinth of Thought

Twisting, turning, mind's embrace,
Poignant memories interlace,
In corridors of dream and taught,
We wander through the labyrinth of thought.

Echoes whisper truths concealed,
In the heart, the wounds unhealed,
Each path we take, a battle fought,
In the silent labyrinth of thought.

Through mazes dark, we seek the light,
To end the endless, timeless flight,
With every twist, a knowledge sought,
In the mystic labyrinth of thought.

Till dawn's first light breaks through the veil,
And secrets lost begin to pale,
Our minds unbound, the dreams are caught,
Released from the labyrinth of thought.

Veil of Self-Discovery

Beneath the stars, where shadows lie,
We glimpse the truths of days gone by,
Behind a veil of night's decree,
Embark on self-discovery.

In mirrors dark, reflections past,
We seek the questions left unasked,
Each fragment tells a history,
Unveiled in self-discovery.

Through valleys deep and mountains high,
Within the silence of a sigh,
We find the place where we are free,
Revealed in self-discovery.

With every step, and every fall,
We learn the truths that shape us all,
Our hearts are keys, the locks set free,
Unlocked through self-discovery.

Hidden Depths of Being

In shadows deep, where thrums the heart,
Secrets whisper, worlds apart,
Veins of mystery, unseen streams,
Guide us through our silent dreams.

Beneath our calm, the ripples play,
Waves of thought, night and day,
Soft reflections, truths to glean,
In hidden depths, we seek the unseen.

A mirrored soul, deep, untold,
In darkness, luminescence holds,
Stories etched in silent cries,
Reveal the depth behind our eyes.

Quiet currents, silent flow,
Through time's weave, their secrets show,
In the still, the whispers grow,
Hidden depths, where spirits go.

Veiled in whispers, cloaked in night,
Our essence lies just out of sight,
In currents deep, we find our being,
Hidden depths, forever seeing.

Revelations of the Soul

Underneath the silent sky,
Lies a truth we can't deny,
Wisdom etched in starlit beams,
Expands within our deepest dreams.

Through the veil of morning light,
The heart reveals its hidden sight,
Sparks of truth in shadows cast,
Show us glimpses of the past.

Oh, the soul, it softly sings,
Through the night, on hidden wings,
Revelations, whisper clear,
Guide us through the webs of fear.

Ancient echoes in the wind,
Secret murmurs, paper-thinned,
In the stillness, voices swell,
Mysteries our hearts compel.

Underneath the cosmic whole,
Lies the depth of every soul,
Bright as stars, past skies unfurled,
Revelations shape our world.

Following the Inner Compass

In the quiet of our mind,
Compass points we hope to find,
Guiding light, a subtle call,
Leads us through the open hall.

Whispers gentle, soft as snow,
Show us paths, where we must go,
Heart's true north, no map can hold,
Inner wisdom, pure and bold.

Silent stars, they light the way,
Through the night, to break of day,
Following the heart's own tune,
Leads us 'neath the silver moon.

Choice by choice, we chart our course,
With heart's compass, silent force,
In its whispers, truth we find,
Guided by our inner mind.

Always onward, journey true,
Through the old to find the new,
Following where whispers lead,
Heart and soul, we intercede.

Inner Harmony's Call

Echoes of a distant chord,
In our hearts, they find accord,
Harmony within the soul,
Guides us to our destined goal.

Melodies of silence hum,
Through the storm, beneath the drum,
In the stillness, hear the call,
Inner peace, the one for all.

Balance sought, in twilight's veil,
Harmony's call will prevail,
Songs of old and future's thread,
In our hearts and in our heads.

Whispers soft through ancient trees,
Carried by the gentle breeze,
Harmony in nature's grace,
Fills our hearts, finds its place.

Songs of peace, forever sung,
In each heart, a bell is rung,
Inner harmony calls us near,
With its truth, so pure and clear.

Charting the Soul's Terrain

Through valleys of doubt, where shadows grow,
We trace the lines, where heartbeats sow.
Across the plains of dreams undone,
We find the path, where hope has spun.

Over mountains high, where courage peaks,
We gather strength, for truth it seeks.
Underneath the stars' embrace,
We find our place, in boundless space.

In forests deep, where whispers dwell,
We listen close, to stories they'll tell.
By rivers clear, that gently wind,
We quench the thirst, of weary mind.

On deserts vast, where silence reigns,
We search for gems, amidst the pains.
In fields of gold, where love is found,
We plant the seeds, in fertile ground.

Through every clime and storm we face,
Our soul's terrain, we bravely trace.
With every step, our journey yields,
A tapestry, that life reveals.

Peering into Inner Waters

Gaze into the depths, where secrets lie,
Reflections cast, beneath the sky.
The silent waves, they gently speak,
Of hidden worlds, the heart does seek.

Beneath the surface, shadows play,
In hues of night, in shades of day.
Echoes of the past, they softly call,
In mirrored ponds, where tears may fall.

Currents carry dreams untold,
In whispered tones, they unfold.
A stream of thought, forever flows,
As mysteries of the soul compose.

Ripples dance on tranquil seas,
Whispering the truths that tease.
In quiet calm, we find our peace,
Inner waters, grant release.

Dive deep within, where fears reside,
In inner waters, truths abide.
With every plunge, we come to see,
The depths of our serenity.

Heart's Secretive Voyage

Sailing on the starlit sea,
Our hearts embark on mystery.
The compass points to lands unknown,
Where whispers of the past are sown.

Crimson sails against the dawn,
The heart's own path it journeys on.
Through tempests fierce and calm lagoons,
It seeks the light of hidden moons.

In coves where dreams and fears entwine,
We grapple with what we may find.
The heart's true north, a subtle guide,
In depths and heights, we must confide.

Amidst the waves of joy and strife,
The heart explores the sea of life.
Anchors raised on shores of grace,
It meets each challenge, face to face.

Only when the journey ends,
The treasure found where love transcends.
The secret maps the heart has drawn,
Reveal a dawn, where fears are gone.

Unraveling Inner Mysteries

Threads of thought, they gently weave,
A tapestry we can't perceive.
Within the mind, where shadows play,
Inner mysteries hold their sway.

Patterns hidden from our sight,
In dreams that stir the silent night.
Through webs of doubt, we slowly tread,
To realms where hidden fears are fed.

In labyrinths of darkest fears,
We wander through our hidden tears.
With every turn, a truth reveals,
The scars and joys our heart conceals.

The key to doors within our soul,
Unlocks the tales that make us whole.
Each revelation, step by step,
Unravels depths we have yet met.

By finding light in shadowed dreams,
We understand what silence means.
Through every mystery explored,
We come to know our own accord.

Mapping Inner Landscapes

Winds of thought do gently blow,
Over valleys deep in mind's low.
Mountains peak with dreams so high,
In the heart's sky, birds do fly.

Paths of memory, rivers flow,
With every step, new buds grow.
Forests thick with secrets laid,
In this map, I'm not afraid.

Echoes whisper through the trees,
Mystery in each soft breeze.
Journey through these mental lands,
Understanding in my hands.

Beyond the cliffs of doubt and fear,
Lies the peace, so bright, so clear.
Navigate with inner light,
Through the day and quiet night.

With each hill and valley crossed,
Find what's there, never lost.
Reflecting on the endless scape,
Mapping thoughts, they take shape.

Silent Conversations with Self

In the quiet of the night,
When the moon is shining bright.
Silent whispers fill the air,
Of thoughts and dreams, laid bare.

Echoes of a mind alone,
Reflecting on what's unknown.
Words unsaid, but understood,
In a realm where all is good.

Shadows dance upon the wall,
Answering the silent call.
Hearts converse in muted tones,
Harmonizing inner zones.

Each pause speaking volumes deep,
Secrets that the silence keeps.
Confiding in the still void,
Complex thoughts, gently employed.

In these talks without a sound,
Many truths, softly found.
Silent prose of self-connect,
Silent love and self-respect.

Fragments of Inner Truth

In the cracks where shadows fall,
Lies fragments of the soul's call.
Pieces scattered, yet so bright,
Shimmering in the soft light.

Truths once hidden, now revealed,
In the heart's core, wounds have healed.
Puzzles forming a whole view,
From the old, emerges new.

Wisdom found in broken shards,
Secrets held in sacred guards.
Past reflections from the glass,
Through the lens, the questions pass.

Gathered pieces, stories told,
New-found strength in self to hold.
Patchwork quilt of inner lore,
Threads of truth restored once more.

Every splinter, every piece,
Forms a harmony of peace.
In the silent broken seams,
Lie the fragments of our dreams.

Embracing the Inner Flame

In the heart's deep burning core,
Lies a flame forevermore.
Warmth that kindles inner light,
Guiding through the darkest night.

Flickers of a passionate glow,
Through the spirit, it does flow.
Fires of determination,
In each breath, a revelation.

Embrace the heat, the fervent blaze,
Through the struggles, through the haze.
Flames of strength and courage rise,
Lighting up the inner skies.

In this fire, pure and bright,
Burns the essence of our fight.
Every ember, every spark,
Lights the way through shadows dark.

Warmth within that never fades,
In its glow, fear slowly wades.
With this flame, embrace the way,
Into dawn from night's gray.

Probing the Inner Silence

In corridors of thought, so bright,
We chase the echoes of the night,
Each shadowed corner holds a clue,
Yet deep inside, we seek the true.

Silence whispers tales long past,
In quiet moments, shadows cast,
A mirrored soul holds truths unknown,
In silence, seeds of wisdom sown.

A heart that listens finds the key,
Unlocking doors to mysteries free,
In silence, answers softly meld,
Within, the sacred truths are held.

Quiet songs of ancient lore,
Within our spirits, gently pour,
The calm embrace of inner peace,
In silence, troubles find release.

As stars in sky of night's expanse,
We find ourselves in silence's dance,
The quiet binds us, soul to mind,
In silent realms, our truths we find.

Wandering through the Self

In meadows of our thoughts, we stroll,
Each flower holds a piece, a whole,
The fragrance of the self so sweet,
In wandering, our spirits meet.

We cross the streams of hopes and dreams,
Reflecting self in sparkling gleams,
Through forests dense with doubts and fears,
The path to self within appears.

Mountains rise in grandeur bold,
With peaks and valleys yet untold,
Each step we take reveals anew,
The essence of what's pure and true.

In caves of introspective quests,
We find our hidden, deepest rests,
Each cavern holds a sway of light,
Defining who we are by right.

A journey through our inner land,
In wandering, we understand,
The self unfolds like petals soft,
In quiet growth, we lift aloft.

Awakening Inner Echoes

In waking dreams, we touch the mind,
Where echoes of our past unwind,
Each memory a lingering trace,
We find our strength in inner grace.

The whispers of the yesteryear,
Resound in hearts when truth is near,
In echoes, we find voices clear,
To guide us through the shadowed fear.

Awakening within our core,
The silent sounds of days before,
Each echo bares a story's thread,
In them, the paths we now are led.

A symphony of inner tunes,
In nights of stars, in noon's bright noons,
These echoes sing of love and loss,
In them we find both gain and cost.

In quiet hours, hearts unfold,
The echoes that our spirits hold,
Awakening the voices past,
We find our truths that ever last.

Inner Wilderness Exploration

Through valleys wild within our minds,
We seek the truths that life defines,
A wilderness of thoughts unchained,
Where secrets of the self are gained.

The rivers of emotion flow,
In currents swift, in eddies slow,
We ride the waves of joy and pain,
Each lesson learned, our wisdom's gain.

Mountains tall of dreams and hope,
We climb their peaks, in wonder grope,
Through vast terrains of doubt and fear,
We chart the paths that bring us near.

Forests deep of untamed thought,
In which the essence must be sought,
In exploration, we find fire,
To fuel our spirits and inspire.

In deserts dry of solitude,
We find the strength in quietude,
An inner realm so wild and vast,
In it, our roots of self are cast.

Retreat into the Core

In the heart of silence's grace,
Where whispers gently trace,
A soulful dance begins to sway,
In light that neither fades nor frays.

Through corridors of ancient thought,
By memories that time forgot,
We find the essence pure, untamed,
In fires that cannot be named.

Beyond the reach of worldly din,
Lies the truth we hold within,
An echo of our deeper ties,
In shadows where the spirit flies.

The burdens of the outer fall,
As inner peace heeds the call,
Within this sanctum, we renew,
In stillness, find the path that's true.

At last, we touch the sacred shore,
In retreat into the core,
Where life's true essence, we embrace,
In hidden depths, we find our place.

Crafting Inner Trails

With every step, a path unfolds,
Through stories that our hearts have told,
In forests deep, and valleys wide,
We journey where our dreams reside.

The trails are marked by quiet streams,
That carry shards of broken dreams,
But in their flow, new hopes emerge,
Crafting trails on life's great verge.

The whispers of the ancient trees,
Dance gently with the evening breeze,
Guiding us through lands unknown,
To places we can call our own.

With each ascent, we come to see,
The visions of our destiny,
In crafting trails, our spirits soar,
To realms unseen, forevermore.

Beneath the stars, we find our way,
Through night into the break of day,
In trails within, our souls entwine,
To the depths of self, divine.

Whispers of Inner Sanctum

In sanctum deep where echoes play,
A tranquil heart begins to sway,
Amongst the murmurs of the soul,
In whispers, we become whole.

The silence sings a timeless song,
In shadows where we all belong,
A melody of mystic light,
That guides us gently through the night.

Within these walls, our spirits soar,
Beyond what eyes have seen before,
In tranquil whispers, soft and clear,
We find the truths we hold most dear.

Each breath we take is pure and free,
In sanctum's grace, a symphony,
Of inner peace newly unfurled,
Embracing both the self and world.

The whispers of our soul's desire,
A gentle veil we now admire,
In sacred space, our spirits mend,
Where inner sanctum has no end.

Embrace of the Inner Shade

In stillness of the twilight's veil,
We journey through a secret trail,
Embracing shade where dreams align,
In shadows cast by heart's design.

The inner shade, a refuge soft,
Where whispered truths are held aloft,
In darkness, light begins to bloom,
Dispelling every worldly gloom.

Amidst the hush of hidden grace,
We find a kinder, gentler place,
Where shadows teach and whisper low,
The truths that only they can show.

Through shade, we see the all unseen,
In places none have ever been,
Embracing depth where light be laid,
Within the heart of inner shade.

In quietude, we come to rest,
Within the shade, our spirits blessed,
Embrace the shadows, do not fade,
In light and dark, forever stayed.

Hidden Arenas

Beneath the veil of twilight's grace,
Lies a world unseen, yet full of trace,
Where shadows dance in a silent race,
And secrets whisper in a hidden space.

Forgotten dreams in a somber field,
Guardians of truth, never to yield,
In silent arenas, their fate is sealed,
Beneath the earth where the heart is healed.

Stars above, witness to plight,
In the hidden realms of endless night,
Battles fought without the light,
In arenas unseen, devoid of sight.

Echoes of courage, lost in time,
In the hidden vastness, they climb,
To unseen summits, so sublime,
In arenas shrouded, freed from grime.

Here lies peace, a silent call,
In hidden arenas, where shadows sprawl,
Lost are the whispers that rise and fall,
In the quiet realms, where secrets enthrall.

Whispers in Solitude

In the quiet corners of the mind,
Where echoes of the past unwind,
A whisper soft, a tale untwined,
In solitude, a truth you'll find.

A breeze that carries silent cries,
In solitude, where silence lies,
Unseen by those with worldly ties,
The whisper sings, the spirit flies.

In dreamy meadows, unseen grace,
In solitude, there's a calm embrace,
A whisper finds a sacred space,
And paints the heart with nature's trace.

The stars above, they hear the plea,
Whispers in solitude, wild and free,
A conversation 'twixt you and the sea,
Bound by the threads of destiny.

Where quiet reigns and hearts commune,
Whispers in solitude, a sweet tune,
In silent nights, beneath the moon,
A whisper speaks, a soul's cocoon.

In the Mirror's Depth

In the mirror's depth, what do you see?
A world obscured, a mystery,
Beyond the glass, an entity,
Reflecting more than eyes can be.

Shadows play in the silver sheen,
Truths unveiled, yet unforeseen,
Within the depths, a silent scene,
Where reality and dreams convene.

A glance reveals, a deeper stare,
A mirrored realm, a world laid bare,
In the depths, no pretense there,
Just the essence of self to share.

Beyond reflections, lies the soul,
In the mirror's depth, a silent scroll,
Written in shadows, yet wholly whole,
The truth beneath, that we patrol.

In the glass, both near and far,
A mirrored dance, like a distant star,
In the mirror's depth, we are
More than what, we think we are.

Echoes Within

In the heart's domain, where echoes dwell,
Silent stories, they weave and swell,
From the depths, they rise and tell,
Tales of a place where shadows fell.

In echoes within, memories linger,
A touch, a breath, light as a finger,
They weave a web of moments, stinger,
In the soul, they softly flinger.

Echoes of laughter, whispers of pain,
In the silent corridors of the brain,
A dance of thoughts, like gentle rain,
Leaking into the heart's domain.

Within each echo, a timeless beat,
Of life's rhythm, so bittersweet,
In the heart's chambers, where worlds meet,
Echoes within, complete the feat.

In solitude, they softly sing,
Echoes within, on quiet wing,
In the heart's depths, they bring,
A symphony of everything.

Reflections on Becoming

In the stillness of the dawn,
Dreams collide with waking thought.
Wisps of what was, nearly gone,
Shape the person time forgot.

From the seeds of yesteryear,
Sprout the future's tender shoot.
In each joy and in each tear,
Lies the truth of one's own root.

Echoes of the past will ring,
Through the corridors of time.
Yet the present, blossoming,
Sings a more profound rhyme.

Through the trials that we face,
And the choices we perceive,
In each moment, a new grace,
In each breath, the right to be.

We are rivers, flowing free,
Merging currents, forging paths.
In becoming, we're at sea,
Anchored only in our hearts.

The Inner Pilgrimage

Journeys traced in endless skies,
Footprints on an unseen trail.
Whispers carried by the sighs,
Of the soul's enduring tale.

Mountains crumbled into dust,
Oceans drained into the earth.
What remains is what we trust,
In the quiet of rebirth.

Mirrors in the mind reflect,
Every shadow, every light.
In these depths we must respect,
Both the darkness and the bright.

Echoes of the soul's old song,
Play within the heart's deep well.
Each note, both serene and strong,
Speaks of truths that words can't tell.

Where the heart and spirit meet,
In the sanctuary rare,
We find paths beneath our feet,
On this journey of the heart.

Beyond the Surface

In the ripples on the pond,
Lies a world of hidden truth.
Much beyond the simple bond,
Of reflection's shallow proof.

Surface mirrors what it sees,
Casting shadows on the light.
Yet beneath, a current frees,
Mysteries of day and night.

In each ripple, stories weave,
Tales of lives unseen, unheard.
Only those who dare believe,
Uncover the whispered word.

Gaze beyond the mirrored sheen,
And the truth will soon take hold.
In the depths, a sight unseen,
Is a story yet untold.

Dive into the depths unknown,
Past the veil of first appeal.
Only when the heart has shown,
Do we see what's truly real.

Into the Mirror of Self

Gaze into the looking glass,
See the face that time has worn.
Reflect on the moments past,
On the self that's been reborn.

Lines and shadows mark the way,
Of a path that's long been trod.
Eyes, the windows to each day,
Glimpse the secrets of the god.

Every scar and every laugh,
Form the tapestry we are.
In the mirror's humble craft,
Lies the light of our own star.

But beneath the surface gleam,
Lives a world not seen by sight.
In our thoughts, like some lost dream,
Float the whispers of the night.

Search within the mirrored soul,
Seek the truth beyond the eye.
In the depths, we find our whole,
Where the heart and spirit lie.

Enigma of the Inner Roads

Whispers of secrets, hidden and old
In labyrinths deep, where shadows unfold
Dreams and fears, entwined like twine
In the corridors of the veiled mind

Steps echo soft, on paths yet unseen
Where light and dark blend in between
Guardians of thoughts, with riddles to say
Guide the seeker through night and day

A heart's compass, though often led blind
Hunts for truths, in paths intertwined
In the silence, where answers bode
Lies the enigma of the inner roads

Mysteries lure in twilight's embrace
With glimmers of hope and traces of grace
Echoes of wisdom, in whispers conveyed
Guide the curious, where shadows played

Celestial lanterns light up the quest
As the soul delves deep in relentless zest
For in the heart, the truth's abode
Unlocks the enigma of the inner roads

Journey to the Inmost

Sailing past shores of shadow and light
Through waves of thought, in day and night
The heart steers brave, to realms unknown
On a journey to the inmost, alone

Veils of illusion, lifted with care
Reveal the spirit's secrets, laid bare
Glimpses of soul in the mirror's glint
Fragments of truth, in hues of tint

With each step closer, bonds are unsealed
Timeless treasures, softly revealed
Imprints of dreams, where memories rest
Guide the seeker, on an eternal quest

Through valleys of silence, past echoes old
The quest unfolds in courage bold
To the deepest parts where truths reside
Led by the heart, with wisdom as guide

The journey within, an endless embrace
Of shadows faced and truths to chase
To the very core, where worlds are entwined
In the sacred journey to the inmost mind

Unveiling the Mystic Within

In the quiet realms where shadows play
Behind the veil of the wakeful day
A mystic realm in the silence resides
Where the soul in solitude confides

Paths of the unknown, ancient and wise
Speak in whispers, with truth in disguise
A journey inward, where answers spin
The quest to unveil the mystic within

Visions unfold in twilight's embrace
Of forgotten dreams, with a delicate grace
Symbols and signs in the whispers hear
Unlocking mysteries held so dear

Through realms of thought and silent tombs
Lies the essence where the spirit blooms
Seeking the light where darkness has been
To uncover the mystic within the skin

A dance with shadows in gentle sway
Leads to dawn of an enlightened day
With each step closer, the revelations begin
In the sacred unveiling of the mystic within

Uncharted Heart's Adventure

The heart's voyage, in dreams embarks
Through uncharted realms and hidden marks
Maps of wonder, unformed and wild
Guide the soul like an untamed child

Journeys through vistas, of silent thought
With treasures of wisdom, in moments caught
In lands unknown, the spirit roves
Through forests of whispers, and silent groves

Winds of destiny, strong and fair
Carry the seeker through realms rare
With faith as compass, hope as strife
Navigating through the maze of life

Unseen horizons, yet to reveal
With every step, the heart does feel
The pulse of truth in a gentle thrall
In the uncharted heart's adventure call

Paths converging, in destiny's flow
Guided by love's eternal glow
To traverse the unknown, and joy venture
On the uncharted heart's adventure

Path to Inner Tranquility

In the whispering winds of dawn,
Lies a peace, so gently drawn.
Beneath the skies of azure blue,
Find a heart that's calm and true.

Among the trees that softly sway,
Stillness leads the soul away.
To realms where thoughts are free to roam,
Crafting silence, sweet as home.

Each breath a symphony in air,
Each step a tribute to the rare.
Where worries fade, and dreams ignite,
In morning's hush, we find our light.

Troubles vanish with the breeze,
Leaving mind and spirit eased.
In tranquil paths of morning grace,
We uncover our sacred space.

Let the quiet be your guide,
In the calmness, gently slide.
For in the silent, humble glow,
Inner peace begins to flow.

Charting Unseen Territories

Beyond the known, there waits a place,
In realms where shadows softly trace.
With starlit maps and hearts that yearn,
Otherworldly paths, we learn.

Brave adventurers of the mind,
In quests unknown, truths we find.
Through veils of night and mists so deep,
Dreams are woven as we sleep.

Oceans vast and skies uncharted,
Where spirits brave become unguarded.
With every step, a story blooms,
In lands obscured by silver moons.

In silence gleams the secret voice,
Guiding those who make the choice.
To venture forth where none have gone,
Seeking wisdom with each dawn.

Boundless are the trails unseen,
In this dance both fierce and serene.
For those who chart these hidden ways,
Discover light beyond the haze.

Uncharted Inner Expedition

Within the depths of our own soul,
Lies a place so rare and whole.
Unmeasured by the world's decree,
A realm of pure discovery.

In silence, whispers softly blend,
Guiding where our truths depend.
Through astral veils and mem'ries vast,
Present futures tied to past.

With courage as our compass here,
We tread unknown without a fear.
Illuminating darkened coasts,
Each new vision gently hosts.

Magic in the quiet found,
With every beat, a sacred sound.
An odyssey within our veins,
Exploring joys and hidden pains.

In shadows of the mind, we seek,
Insights deep, both lush and meek.
For uncharted inner lands do show,
The truths that we have yet to know.

Illumination of the Heart

In the stillness of the night,
Lies a flame both pure and bright.
Guiding spirits through the dark,
With a soft, unwavering spark.

Moments fleeting, shadows part,
Touched by light within the heart.
Every beat a beacon clear,
Lighting paths both far and near.

In the glow of inner peace,
Worldly fears and troubles cease.
Silent pulses, truths reveal,
While the soul begins to heal.

Connected to the cosmic beat,
Universal love we greet.
With open hearts and minds profound,
In this light we're ever bound.

Let the luminance freely flow,
In its warmth, forever grow.
For in the heart's eternal gleam,
We find the essence of our dream.

Navigating the Soul's Maze

In corridors where shadows dance,
We navigate the cryptic trance,
Through winding paths and mystic haze,
Exploring life's enchanted ways.

Whispers guide us in the night,
Through darkened roads, to dawn's first light,
Inward journeys, hearts confined,
Seeking truths our minds can't find.

Silent echoes from the past,
Memories that hold us fast,
Footsteps tread on ancient ground,
Seeking solace, souls unbound.

Labyrinths of thought unwind,
In the maze, we seek, we find,
Fragments of a fractured dream,
Glimpses of the soul's esteem.

Every turn reveals anew,
Mysteries that life imbues,
In this maze where hearts contend,
From the start until the end.

Exploring Hidden Essence

Beneath the veil, the essence lies,
Hidden from the prying eyes,
Depths of spirit, depths of mind,
Truths concealed, yet intertwined.

Whispered secrets, softly told,
Wisdom wrapped in tales of old,
Through the quiet, through the still,
Seeking dreams that hearts fulfill.

Mystic realms within us soar,
Unseen worlds at our core,
Every thread of thought unwinds,
Leading to the hidden finds.

Silent rivers, deeply flow,
Where our truest spirits go,
In the stillness, life reveals,
All the truths that silence heals.

Journey inward, journey deep,
In the shadows, secrets keep,
Seeking essence, finding peace,
In the heart's own sweet release.

Heartland's Secret Tracks

Hidden paths through meadows green,
Silent trails by eyes unseen,
In the heartland, secrets laid,
In the quiet, truths conveyed.

Softly tread where no one knows,
Follow where the wild wind blows,
In the stillness, hear the call,
Of the heartland, over all.

Echoes of a time gone by,
In the seed and in the sky,
Footsteps on the ancient track,
Lead us forth, and guide us back.

Nature's whispers in the breeze,
Heartland's voice through rustling trees,
Every leaf and every stone,
Speaks of secrets all its own.

Journey through this sacred space,
Find a path, find your place,
In the heartland, in its grace,
Feel the earth's tender embrace.

Inner Reverie's Voyage

Within the mind's expansive sea,
Waves of dream and memory,
Sail the currents, deep and wide,
On this inner reverie's tide.

Thoughts like stars in heavens vast,
Shimmer through the night's contrast,
Guiding journeys, inward gleam,
Through the landscape of a dream.

Silent realms where echoes call,
Murmurs of the soul's heartfall,
Charting paths through unseen streams,
Voyaging through hidden themes.

Every whisper, every sigh,
Winds us through the inward sky,
In the silence, find the song,
Of the place where we belong.

Boundless voyages in flight,
Through the day and through the night,
Inner worlds and cosmic ways,
On this reverie's endless maze.

Soul's True Compass

Beneath the stars, we wander, lost,
In endless night, our spirits tossed.
Yet deep within, the needle points,
To realms where peace and hope anoints.

The heart, a map, to guide the way,
Through shadows cast by doubt's array.
In silent whispers, truth confides,
Where compass leads, the soul abides.

Across the storms of life's deceit,
The true north calls, a steady beat.
Through valleys dark and peaks so high,
The inner light will never lie.

In sacred stillness, heed the call,
To trust the path, to stand, not fall.
When lost, but listening close, refine,
The compass draws the perfect line.

In twilight's glow, the journey starts,
With faith and courage in our hearts.
Though tempests rage and winds may roar,
The compass guides forevermore.

Ancient Inner Pathways

Beneath the ancient trees we tread,
On pathways paved by souls long dead.
Whispers soft, from roots adored,
Guide us to a hidden accord.

Each step a link to yesteryears,
Echoes of laughter, silent tears.
The past and present intertwine,
In shadows cast, the spirits sign.

The moss-clad stones, a tale retold,
Of journeys braved by hearts so bold.
Through time and space, the soul aligns,
With ancient paths, the spirit shines.

The whispering winds, the rustling leaves,
A symphony that time conceives.
In quiet moments, we embrace,
The secret paths, the sacred space.

In twilight's cusp, we find our way,
Guided by what the ancients say.
Through alleys dark, through dawn's first light,
The pathways lead to wisdom's height.

Rebirth of the Inner Light

In shadows deep, where spirits dwell,
A spark ignites, begins to swell.
The inner light, though dimmed by night,
Awakens from the darkest plight.

Through trials harsh and tempests dire,
The flame within, it does not tire.
In moments bleak, of endless shade,
The light revives, our fears allayed.

Emerging from the ashen grey,
A phoenix rises in the fray.
Its wings unfurl, in glowing fire,
To heavens high, it does aspire.

With every breath, the embers glow,
In quiet strength, from depths below.
Revived, renewed, our spirits soar,
To realms where shadows touch no more.

In dawn's embrace, we greet the light,
With hearts reborn from endless night.
Through brokenness, the soul aright,
In radiant hope, completes its flight.

Understanding the Unseen

In quiet depths, where shadows play,
The unseen world begins to sway.
With whispered hints, it draws us near,
Beyond the veil of sight and fear.

In silence deep, the secrets weave,
A tapestry we scarce believe.
The eyes may miss, but heart will see,
The truth that dwells in mystery.

The unseen binds, the fabric tight,
Of dreams and thoughts beyond our sight.
In soft embrace, it breathes around,
In every pulse, in every sound.

To understand what lies concealed,
We must, in stillness, find the field.
In soul's retreat, with senses keen,
The unseen world is deeply seen.

In twilight's grace, where shadows bend,
Perceptions meld, and truths transcend.
To comprehend, to bridge the rift,
We see the unseen's precious gift.

Echoed Reflections

In the quiet of the stream,
Ripples dance on mirrored gleam.
Waves of moments, time forgot,
Nature's echo, untied knot.

Silent whispers in the wind,
Memories of what has been.
Reflections tell in fleeting light,
Stories hidden in the night.

Skies above, a canvas gray,
Painted with the break of day.
Echoes fade, yet still remain,
In a heart that bears no chain.

Footsteps in the sand, erased,
By the tide's relentless chase.
Yet the soul remembers all,
Echoes' silent, distant call.

Gaze into the mirrored deep,
Where the past and present sleep.
Echoes of a life entwined,
In reflections we can find.

Finding the Silent Voice

In a world of endless noise,
Find the space where silence toys.
Whispers of a hidden truth,
Known since days of fleeting youth.

Silent songs of nature's choir,
Words unspoken, hearts aspire.
Listen close and you will hear,
Voice inside, so pure and clear.

Amidst the clamor, still a sphere,
Where your thoughts become sincere.
Echoes of your inner song,
Guide you through, where you belong.

Gentle murmurs of the breeze,
Rustling leaves among the trees.
Silent voice within you, speak,
Strength is found within the meek.

Embrace the quiet, let it grow,
Seeds of wisdom, thought will sow.
Find the voice that silence breeds,
In the calm, your spirit feeds.

Masks of Me

Behind the mask, a tale untold,
Facades of strength, a heart of gold.
Eyes that shimmer, veiled in light,
Truth that's hidden from our sight.

Masked in laughter, tears conceal,
Depths of pain, a scar to heal.
Voices lost in crowded space,
Show the world a different face.

Layers thick, as time endures,
Masks protect, but also lures.
Veils of sorrow, hues of pride,
In this dance, the true selves hide.

Each mask crafted, worn with care,
Yet the soul remains laid bare.
Glimpses through the cracks we see,
Fragments of the true and free.

Remove the mask, if just for now,
Let the world see where and how.
In the honest, bare expanse,
Your true self shall there enhance.

Inward Pilgrimage

Journeys taken not by feet,
Inner paths, a quest discreet.
Roads unmarked by sign or stone,
Destinations still unknown.

Each step inward, closer still,
Mountains of the mind to will.
Valleys deep and rivers wide,
Cross within, no bounds outside.

Pilgrimage to self and soul,
Pieces searching to be whole.
Silent prayers, thoughts confessed,
Journey to the heart's own quest.

Maps of old and stories told,
Guide the spirit, pure and bold.
Inward glances, realizing,
Truths within us, harmonizing.

Ending where we first began,
Understanding the simple plan.
Pilgrimage within shall show,
All we need, and all we know.

Inner Visionary Walk

Through winding trails of thought, we go,
Past dreams that whisper, ebb and flow,
In shadows cast by fears we cloak,
A light of truth begins to glow.

Along the path of self-discovery,
Each step reveals another key,
To unlock visions deep within,
Unfolding our true destiny.

The whispers guide, the heart aligns,
To realms unseen, the spirit finds,
A place where soul and mind converge,
In harmony, their dance unwinds.

With every stride, we gather grace,
To face the world, its fierce embrace,
And in this walk of inner sight,
We find our center, our rightful place.

So wander on, through thoughts so vast,
In present dreams, and echoes past,
For in this journey, we shall find,
The visionary self, unmasked.

Ripples of Inner Sea

Within the quiet of the mind,
Lie waters deep, and secrets find,
The ripples form with every thought,
Reflecting dreams that we have sought.

Each wave is born of silent sighs,
Beneath the tranquil, Azure skies,
They carry whispers on their crest,
A journey to the soul's behest.

The echoes ripple far and near,
Stirring hopes and calming fear,
In stillness, currents start to flow,
To worlds within, we let them go.

Beneath the surface, oceans hide,
The treasures of our inner tide,
And as we dive, the truth reveals,
The depths of self, where spirit heals.

On this voyage, through our sea,
We find the calm, the mystery,
And in the ripples' soft caress,
Embrace the soul's profound finesse.

Journey of Hidden Paths

Through forests dense, and valleys deep,
We walk the trails our hearts do keep,
In shadows cast by ancient trees,
The whispers call, a timeless plea.

The hidden paths, by moonlight shown,
Are mapped by dreams we call our own,
With every step, a world unveiled,
A silent quest where souls ingenue.

In labyrinths of thought we tread,
The silent whispers we are led,
Each turn reveals a spark of light,
Guiding us through endless night.

These paths of mystery, they wind,
Through realms of heart and soul combined,
And in each step, we find our place,
A journey bathed in glowing grace.

So walk the trails of hidden lore,
Discover what was lost before,
For in these paths, the heart does see,
The journey leads to true, to thee.

Pathway to Serene Self

Among the fields where wildflowers sing,
A pathway calls with gentle ring,
A trail that leads to inner peace,
Where heart and mind find sweet release.

In silence, footsteps tread so light,
Through whispers of the dawning light,
The breeze, it dances, soft and free,
Unraveling serenity.

Each step, a whisper to the soul,
In quest to make the self-hood whole,
Through valleys deep and mountains high,
The spirit soars, begins to fly.

This journey, one of quiet grace,
To find the self, embrace its space,
To touch the depths where peace unfolds,
And bask in warmth so calm it holds.

So walk this pathway, calm and clear,
With every step, draw ever near,
To the serene, the still, the true,
The self that's waiting, just for you.

Secret Paths of Mind

In hidden corners shadows play,
Where thoughts in silence find their way.
A whisper here, a secret sigh,
In depths where mysteries lie.

Footsteps soft on paths unknown,
By moon's faint light they softly roam.
A dance of dreams in silent night,
Where whispers echo distant flight.

Steps of wonder, paths untold,
Secrets woven, brave and bold.
Through the mist of thought they weave,
Intricate and hard to perceive.

The mind a labyrinth so deep,
In its folds memories steep.
Hidden truths in corners lie,
On silent paths where dreams fly.

In these realms of thought and time,
Mysteries and wonders climb.
Secret paths that wind and twist,
In the shadows, they exist.

Trail of Inner Whispers

A murmur soft, a gentle plea,
Through the heart it wanders free.
Silent echoes in the night,
Guiding us with unseen light.

Voices soft from places deep,
Secrets they are sworn to keep.
On the trail where whispers tread,
Follow where the soul is led.

The quiet hum of thoughts at play,
In the corners roadways stray.
Inner voices, soft and true,
Lead the way when skies are blue.

Paths of silence, paths of grace,
Taken at a measured pace.
Where the heart's soft whispers lead,
Follows soul's most tender need.

In the stillness, hear the call,
Guiding spirit, guiding all.
Follow whisper, follow thread,
On the trail by heartstrings led.

Soul's Sacred Journey

Among the stars the soul takes flight,
In realms that glow of purest light.
Sacred paths the soul does tread,
In the spaces dreams are fed.

Beneath the sky so vast and wide,
Where silent truths and secrets hide.
The journey sacred, long and deep,
In realms where angels softly weep.

Each step imbued with sacred fire,
Carving paths of pure desire.
Through the night and through the stars,
Boundless journeys leave no scars.

Whispers of the soul unfold,
Mysteries and stories told.
In the shadows, in the light,
Soul's journey, sacred, free in flight.

In the quiet, hear the sound,
Of the sacred all around.
Journey deep and journey far,
Soul's adventure, shining star.

Unspoken Inner Wanderings

In the lands of unspoken dreams,
Where thoughts flow like gentle streams.
Silent paths the heart explores,
In places whispered thoughts adore.

Wandering through the fields of mind,
Treasures hidden, hard to find.
In the quiet, truths arise,
Underneath the boundless skies.

Silent journeys, deep and pure,
Through the heart's corridors sure.
Unspoken dreams and wanderings,
On the soul's soft fluttering wings.

Pathways winding, soft and slow,
Inner landscapes gently glow.
Wanderings of heart and soul,
In lands where secret whispers roll.

In the stillness, in the night,
Unspoken thoughts take gentle flight,
Guided by the inner light,
On wanderings with dreams alight.

9 789916 860564